SILENT CITIES

NORMAN F CARVER JR

Books by Norman F. Carver, Jr:

FORM AND SPACE OF JAPANESE ARCHITECTURE
SILENT CITIES (1965 edition)
ITALIAN HILLTOWNS
IBERIAN VILLAGES
JAPANESE FOLKHOUSES

NORMAN F CARVER JR

SILENT CITIES

OF MEXICO AND THE MAYA

DOCUMAN PRESS LTD

ACKNOWLEDGEMENTS

Many institutions and individuals offered assistance both during preliminary investigations and in the field. A complete list would be long, but I owe particular thanks to Harvard and the University of Michigan for access to their archaeological collections; to Dr. William Coe and Ron Calvert for their help and advice; to the guides at Hacienda Uxmal in the 60's for their patience in showing me unknown places; and especially to Sue Parish, who recently, with bush-pilot skill, flew me to the sites for up-to-date photographs and aerials. In Yucatan I must thank Fernando and Carmen Barbachano for their gracious hospitality; the Desarrollo Touristico's Alicia de Blanco and Daniel Navarette for timely and friendly assistance. I owe most, however, to my wife Joan who encouraged me to do this new edition and whose perceptive critiques and plain hard work helped bring it to completion.

PREFACE

Preparation of SILENT CITIES involved more than five years of research and travel to sites in Mexico, Guatemala, and Honduras. Out of hundreds of photographs made 170 were selected, which together with 14 site plans, illustrate sixteen architecturally important Pre-Columbian cities. The cities are grouped according to their Mexican or Mayan origins, and within each group they follow a rough chronological sequence. Periods of active occupation are shown in the chart in the Table of Contents. The dates are approximate and continually being revised by new discoveries.

To help visualize and compare the broad composition of the cities, sketch plans have been included that show the cities as they existed in their classic phases. The plans are based on existing surveys, maps, photographs, visits—and some guesses. All are at the same scale (one inch = 100 meters) and at the same orientation (North towards the top of the page), except for Teotihuacan where the scale has been halved to fit the page. Traditional names for buildings and sites, usually supplied by the Spanish, generally have been retained even though many are inaccurate appellations. Key letters on the plans and legends identify the buildings illustrated or discussed.

Documan Press, Ltd.
Post Office Box 387
Kalamazoo, MI 49005

ISBN: 0-932076-06-8 Cloth
ISBN: 0-932076-07-6 Paper

Designed by Norman F. Carver, Jr.
Printed by Dai Nippon Ltd.
Printed in Japan

CONTENTS

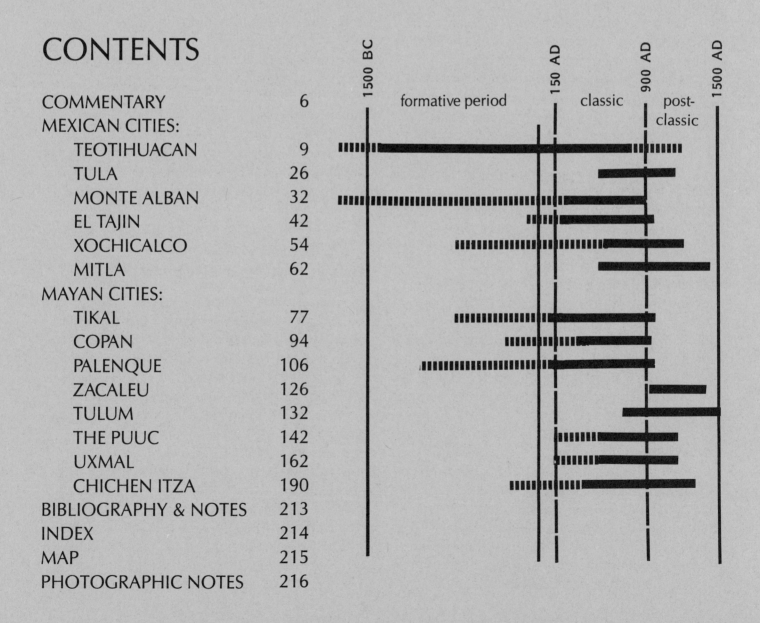

1500 BC   150 AD   900 AD   1500 AD

formative period   classic   post-classic

COMMENTARY

The first edition of this book grew out of my realization that the visual drama of these ancient cities had for too long been buried by excessive archaeological and historical detail and that, vitiated by stereotyped photographs, these powerful forms had been reduced to mere anecdotes of vanished civilizations.

My presentation, therefore, is primarily visual. Although these cities and their architecture exist today only as partially restored ruins, the photographs attempt to evoke some sense of the original architectural concepts although not entirely ignoring the appeal of the picturesque, that blending of the intentional and the accidental that is the essence of these now silent cities.

The cultural background of this architecture has been the subject of many books and is only briefly sketched here. Although knowledge of its historical-cultural context may seem necessary for the appreciation of a work of architecture, such knowledge may diffuse its visual impact. For architectural form is essentially abstract and its fundamental expressive qualities exist independent of its cultural motivations. Motivations may be intriguing but they contribute little to the immediate enjoyment of exhilarating space or form. Knowing that Chartre Cathedral was built in the Gothic style is not what makes ones spine tingle standing in the nave.

Furthermore, a cultural and temporal distance, by divesting architecture of its practical and representative life, heightens abstraction and aids in direct perception of form. In addition, as George Kubler has pointed out, "the work of art is incapable of being made to explain a culture in which it was produced. No explanation of culture ever fully accounts for its works of art because aesthetic activity lies in part outside culture...and is a possible agent in its change."[1]

Art and architecture as a force in cultural change is an idea that seldom occurs to those engaged in cataloguing the minutiae of cultural influences. The sudden appearance of new forms is often seized upon as evidence of major cultural or military intrusions when it may simply have been a bored Mayan architect visiting a neighboring land and returning eager to astound his patron with new discoveries. From such simple circumstances can come powerful change—witness the far reaching influence of Chinese architecture on Japanese building without benefit of military conquest or wholesale social contact. In an area as crisscrossed by traders as Middle America, the possibility of architectural innovations arising out of individual effort is real, yet seldom recognizable.

Origins

For centuries after discovery and settlement of the Americas the existence of these ancient cities was either unknown or ignored. At the time of the Spanish conquest in 1521 most were already in ruins or swallowed by the jungle. Only a few individuals knew they existed or sensed their importance and extent. Little investigation occurred until the 19th century. The man most responsible for arousing interest was an American, John Lloyd Stephens, who traveled through Central America and Yucatan in the 1840's and returned to write best-selling accounts of his discoveries. Coming to his task after extensive travels in the Greek and Egyptian world he speculated with some authority and surprising accuracy on the origins and significance of what he saw. The present book includes several apt descriptions and comments by Stephens as well as those by a late 19th century European visitor, Desire Charnay, who left an interesting if sometimes provincial account.

The origins of New World civilizations have been the subject of much speculation being ascribed to every ancient source from Egyptian to Polynesian. Undoubtedly there were scattered contacts with several parts of the Old World, but investigation confirms that America was originally peopled by Asians moving across the Bering Straits during the interglacial periods from ten to fifty thousand years ago with few contacts since. After thousands of years of nomadic existence, the city building Mexican-Mayan cultures, as well as others, began emerging during the millennium or two before Christ.

The cities did not suddenly appear—instead, like cities everywhere, they were built and re-built over hundreds of years buffeted by the changing fortunes of their inhabitants and the ambitions of their leaders. In recognition of this evolutionary process, archaeologists have organized Mesoamerican development into four main periods. These periods are outlined below with a brief description of important events. All dates in this book are based on the Goodman-Thompson correlation of Mayan and Christian calendars, the one most generally accepted and increasingly confirmed by the carbon-14 method of measuring radio active decay of organic materials.

FORMATIVE PERIOD, 1500 BC to 150 AD

Rise of agricultural civilizations based on maize (corn) and beans. Similar cultural and religious organization throughout the area. Later, the development of a priest caste, and Mayan hieroglyphics and calendar. First construction at Teotihuacan, Monte Alban, and in Guatemala.

CLASSIC PERIOD, 150 AD to 900 AD

Slow differentiation of cultures. Important advances in hieroglyphic and astronomical skills. Establishment and maturation of typical architectural forms. Continually changing dominance of culture and cities.

POST-CLASSIC PERIOD, 900 AD to 1500 AD

Barbarian invasions of the Mexican plateau. Rise of the Toltecs and their invasion of Yucatan. Political strife and the decline of building activity. Complete, and apparently sudden abandonment of major cities, especially by the Mayans. Spanish conquest 1518-1521.

Building Technology

Technologically in the stone age, early Americans built without the use of the wheel or metal tools. The principal materials for their monumental structures were stone (volcanic stone in the Mexican highlands and easily quarried limestone in the Mayan area), a kind of cement, and stucco made by burning limestone.

Initially a rough facing on rubble mounds, the stone was covered with thick stucco, painted with designs in bright colors. As masonry skills increased, the stone was used decoratively and covered with thinner stucco, though still painted. Finally at Mitla, the stonework is so skillful stucco was almost entirely eliminated (62ff).

Although most building types and construction techniques were similar, the Mexican and Mayan methods of enclosing interior space were fundamentally different. Now long since disappeared, pole structures with thatched roofs or flat roofs of beams covered with plaster were typical in Mexico and at Toltec Chichen Itza. This permitted large rooms and even colonnaded halls such as the

Continued on page 73   7

PART I

MEXICAN CITIES
TEOTIHUACAN
TULA
MONTE ALBAN
EL TAJIN
XOCHICALCO
MITLA

The stylized design of this huge tablet, now at the Anthropological Museum, is characteristic of the early Classic Period (150-300 AD) in Teotihuacan culture (9).

TEOTIHUACAN

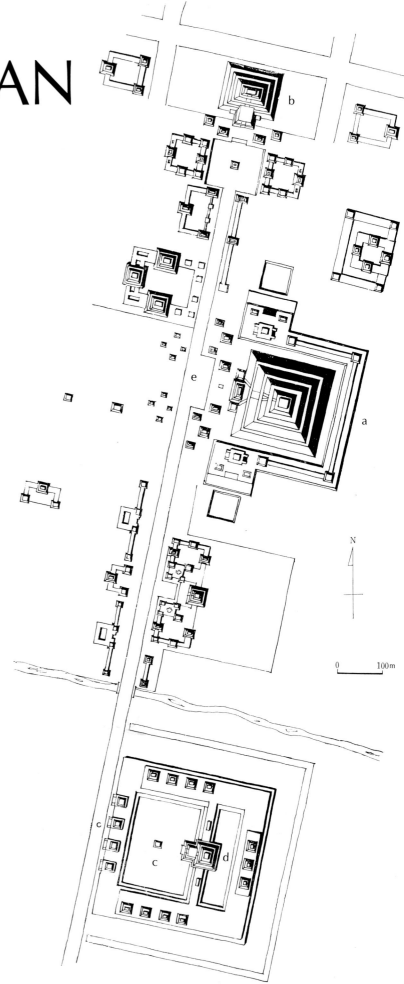

This most impressively scaled of all New World cities appears not only to have been the first major urban complex but also a major cultural influence throughout Middle America for over fifteen hundred years. Probably of Nahautl origin from the time of Christ, Teotihuacan's later cultural sequences are unclear, though its imprint is found on cities from pre-Classic Kaminaljuyu in Guatemala to post-Classic Chichen Itza.

From the beginning, its miles of axial geometry anchored by the huge pyramids were the focus for all central Mexico. The effects must have been stunning for even now the Pyramid of the Sun, though stripped of its stucco and color, is an awesome sight across the bleak plateau. The Avenue of the Dead, the major axis, seems to have been established early and ordered all subsequent building. Surrounding this vast ceremonial center were more than nine square miles of city laid out in a grid pattern. The plan, (shown at half the scale of the other plans because of its immense size) is the most rigorously organized of any Pre-Columbian city.

a Pyramid of the Sun

b Pyramid of the Moon

c The Citadel

d Temple of Quetzalcoatl

e Avenue of the Dead

Orientation appears based on the Sun Pyramid's alignment with the setting sun on the two days a year the sun is at its zenith—and a north-south axis which passes through a cleft in the mountain range to the north, where a small group of ruins has been discovered (12-13). The power of this axis and the significance of its orientation imbues Teotihuacan with an unusually strong sense of order felt even in detail.

The architectural elements of the composition are simple and few, varying only slightly from group to group. The axial arrangement imposes a comprehensive order that emphasizes the relationships between the static, contained shapes with their rhythmically echoing forms. Teotihuacan is a vast geometricized landscape of insistent horizontals punctuated by two massive pyramids.

The Pyramid of the Sun is the largest pyramid in the New World despite losing more than 20 feet of its outer covering on all but the main facade during restoration in the early part of this century. The monumental steps on the west face originally led to a small thatched temple on the peak. In 1971 a cave was accidentally discovered directly beneath the pyramid. The site of ancient religious rites, the cave must have determined the pyramid's location and orientation (11-15).

Stepped platforms consisting of recessed vertical walls above a sloped base (termed talud-tablero) endlessly repeat, with only slight variation, in Teotihuacan's monumental structures. Sections of the thick, painted stucco which once covered the volcanic masonry still cling here and there (12-13, 16,17).

The sculptured facade of an early temple to Quetzalcoatl, the ubiquitous god of middle American cultures. Here, the feathered serpent alternates with what resembles Tlaloc, the rain god. At the center of a complex known as the Citadel, the Temple is flanked by newly uncovered residential groups, leading some to regard the Citadel as the palace of Teotihuacan's rulers (18-19).

From the Pyramid of the Moon looking south towards the Sun Pyramid and the Citadel beyond. The city and the surrounding villages, with a population of approximately 200,000 at their height, spread across the valley floor.

The Avenue of the Dead at the base of the Pyramid of the Moon is lined with recently restored temple platforms—probably people thronged the avenue much as occurs any Sunday today.

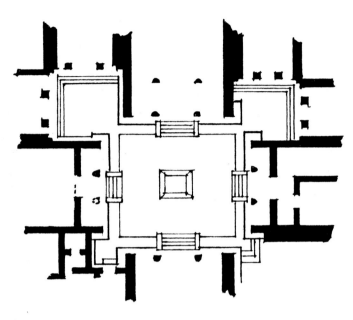

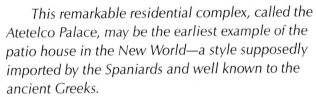

This remarkable residential complex, called the
Atetelco Palace, may be the earliest example of the
patio house in the New World—a style supposedly
imported by the Spaniards and well known to the
ancient Greeks.

But more ingenious than the typical Mediterranean
patio, Atetelco's arrangement of smaller patios
opening off the corners of the main courtyard (see
plan above) gives all rooms or apartments access to
light and air.

Some distance west of Teotihuacan's ceremonial
center, these houses (or palaces or apartments) were
lavishly painted with brilliantly colored murals, some
of which have been found well preserved. The columns
supporting the flat roofs were intricately carved, further
indicating that these were not the quarters of common
folk (24).

TULA

Despite its unimpressive remains, Tula is now regarded as the fabled capital of the vigorous Toltecs who ruled most of central Mexico and later Yucatan for two and a half centuries. The nearby and vastly more appropriate Teotihuacan had once seemed the likely capital, but the wide disparity between these two cities is undoubtedly explained by the barbarian background of the Toltecs and their short, turbulent history. Moreover, Tula was sacked and burned, then much of its sculpture looted by the Aztecs for reuse in their buildings.

Although the Toltecs appear to have possessed some metal tools, their building techniques and level of refinement are modest. However, their god-king, driven out of Tula in AD 987 in a factional conflict, conquered much of Yucatan, where in combination with Mayan sensitivity Toltec achievements outweigh those in their own capital.

The most impressive aspect of Tula today is the group of Atlantean figures standing forlornly atop the Quetzalcoatl Pyramid; but the effect is misleading since the figures were originally columns supporting the roof of a walled temple. Other remains of sculpture and friezes are remarkably similar to, if more excellently executed at, Chichen Itza.

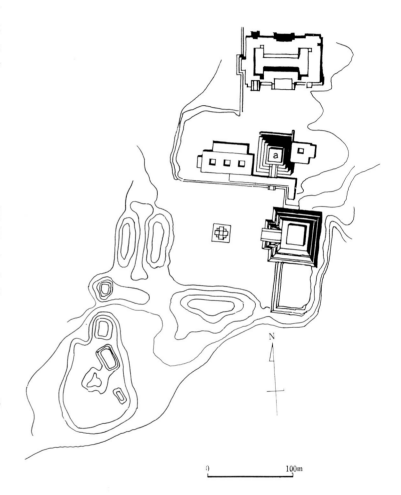

0   100m

a   Temple of Quetzalcoatl

b   Atlantean Columns

c   The Market

26

A wall decorated with geometric patterns and skulls near the main pyramid (27).

Entrance to the Temple atop the pyramid led through a large colonnaded structure which may have been a market or ceremonial hall for festivals that drew the peasants to this capital from all over the highlands. A similar, better preserved structure, also surrounded by a 'market', can be seen in the Toltec-Maya Temple of the Warriors at Chichen Itza (202, 206-209).

On examining the monuments at Tula, we are filled with admiration for the marvelous building capacity of the people who erected them; for, unlike most primitive nations, they used every material at once. They coated their inner walls with mud and mortar, faced their outer walls with baked bricks and cut stone, had wooden roofs, and brick and stone staircases. They were acquainted with pilasters (we found them in their houses), with caryatids, with square and round columns; indeed they seem to have been familiar with every architectural device. That they were painters and decorators we have ample indications in the house we unearthed, where the walls are covered with rosettes, palms, red, white, and gray geometrical figures on a black ground. (Desire Charnay, 1887)

Atlantean columns atop the pyramid originally supported the Temple roof (30, 31).

MONTE ALBAN

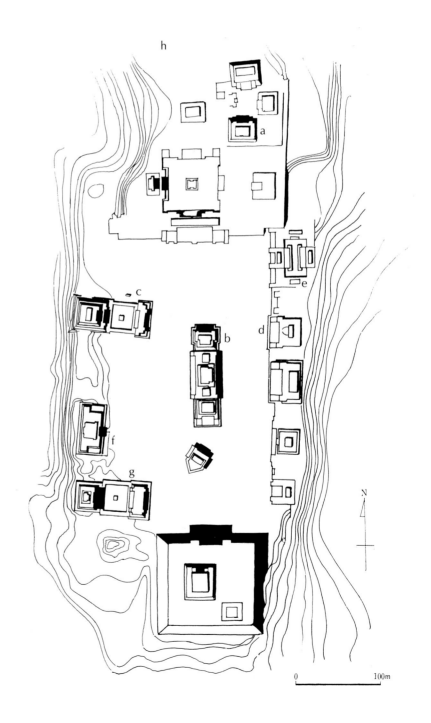

a North mound

b Central Pyramid

c System IV

d East temple stairs

e Ball Court

f Panels of the Dancers

g Group M

h Tomb 104

0 _____ 100m

Monte Alban's commanding position on an isolated group of hills at the juncture of several fertile valleys is undoubtedly responsible for its settlement in pre-historic times. The earliest recorded period, Monte Alban I, from 700 to 300 BC has left only the panels of the dancers. The buildings visible today are of the much later Classic Zapotec period of Monte Alban III B, from 500 to 1000 AD.

Over the centuries the central hills were sculpted into an acropolis of plazas, pyramids, platforms. The casual axiality of the North, Central and South mounds seems to be partly the result of using existing rock outcroppings. Two nearby hills contain small groups of structures, and scattered about the hillsides are hundreds of small residential terraces and 170 tombs—some found intact with treasures of gold, silver, and jade (41).

The individual forms at Monte Alban reflect some of the undecorated simplicity and rhythmic horizontality of Teotihuacan. However, lines and planes do not simply wrap around corners, but are manipulated and projected to emphasize their hovering quality, strengthen the authority of line, and sharpen the silhouette—effects surely enhanced by the original stucco finish.

Monte Alban is an example of the early realization by Mexican builders that articulated, exaggerated and bold geometry were required to effectively distinguish their massive masonry forms from the natural mounds and hills of their settings.

Detail of Temple showing the articulated corners so typical of this Zapotec site (33).

The entire acropolis at dawn seen from a northern mound (34-35).

The central pyramid and System IV on the west edge of the acropolis (36). Stairways along the east edge of the main plaza led to a series of small temples (37).

Details of the cluster known as Group M and the Ball Court (38, 39).

The single figures are two of the many carved panels from Monte Alban I—the so called dancers (more likely the corpses of vanquished warriors) which once faced a temple base. The third fragment may depict a procession of warriors in full regalia. Undisturbed Tomb 104, unearthed north of the plaza, contained the remains of its occupant, gold jewelry, murals on the tomb walls, and this ceramic figure in a niche above the entrance (41).

EL TAJIN

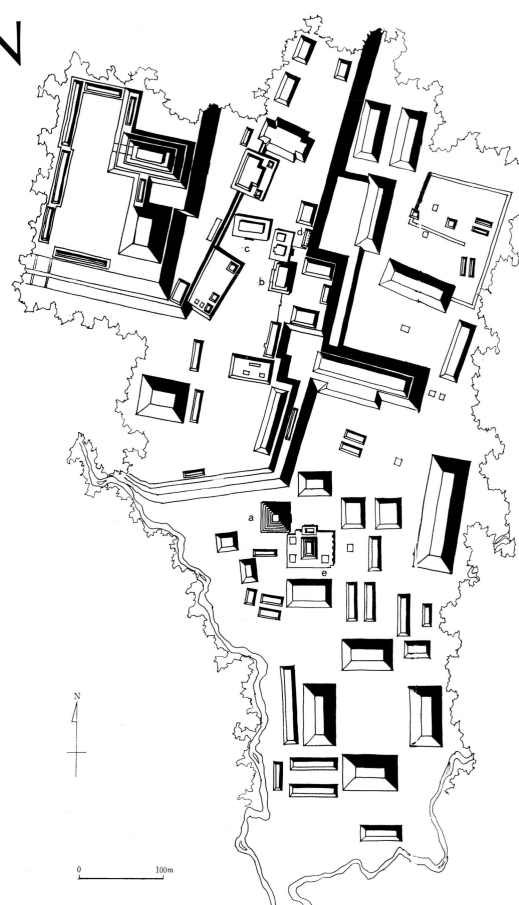

a Pyramid of the Niches

b Tajin Chico, Pyramid

c Tajin Chico, plaza

d Tajin Chico, platform base

e Ball Court bas-relief

N

0   100m

El Tajin, a large important site abandoned to the jungle long before the Conquest, remained unknown until the end of the 18th century. Only recently has a large area been cleared of jungle and some restoration begun. Adapted to the softer light of the rainy Gulf Coast, the architecture of Tajin is a highly expressive version of highland Mexican forms. The sixty-foot Pyramid of the Niches is among the most boldly sculptured masses in the New World. Its widely flared cornices and deeply set niches establish an insistent silhouette and expressive surface in sunlight or mist.

The northern half of the site, called Tajin Chico or Lesser Tajin, is from a somewhat later period. Juxtaposed around its central plaza are a vigorously contoured, truncated pyramid and restrained facades apparently derived from Puuc-Mayan architecture.

Detail of the stairway balustrade from the Temple of the Niches (43).

Small but intricately detailed, the Temple of the Niches contains 365 recesses, one for each day of the year. The surrounding structures, echoing the pyramid, create a rhythmic interplay of angled walls and projecting cornices (44-48).

Lesser Tajin (49-52) combines elements of bold Tajin geometry in the platform base (49) and pyramid facade (51b, 52) with the restrained Mayan-style walls around the plaza (50, 51t).

Elegantly carved panels from the South Ball Court portray human sacrifice. With their low-relief and controlled flowing lines, they are among the choicest sculpture produced in ancient America and in marked contrast to the generally chiaroscuro atmosphere of Tajin (53).

XOCHICALCO

a Temple of Quetzalcoatl
b Ball Court

This hilltop, dominating a pleasant valley to the south and west and arid plains to the north, was initially occupied about 700 AD. Over the years it was transformed into a series of terraces and plazas, punctuated here and there by small pyramids, platforms and ball courts. Despite the extended development and immensity of the task, the result is an orderly arrangement with apparent hieratic and defensive significance.

The most interesting architecture so far restored is the small platform illustrated. The unusual sculpting of the sloping base is a representation of the feathered serpent god Quetzalcoatl. The Classic Mayan feeling of this platform and its decoration indicate to some historians an intrusion of the Maya into the central plateau, heralding the later Toltec-Mayan confluence in Yucatan.

Panorama to the south with the Ball Court in the foreground.

The Temple of Quetzalcoatl, named for the feathered serpent coiled around its base, reverses the standard elements of pre-Columbian talud-tablero platforms— the normally small, plain base here dominates the composition (55, 58, 60-61).

MITLA

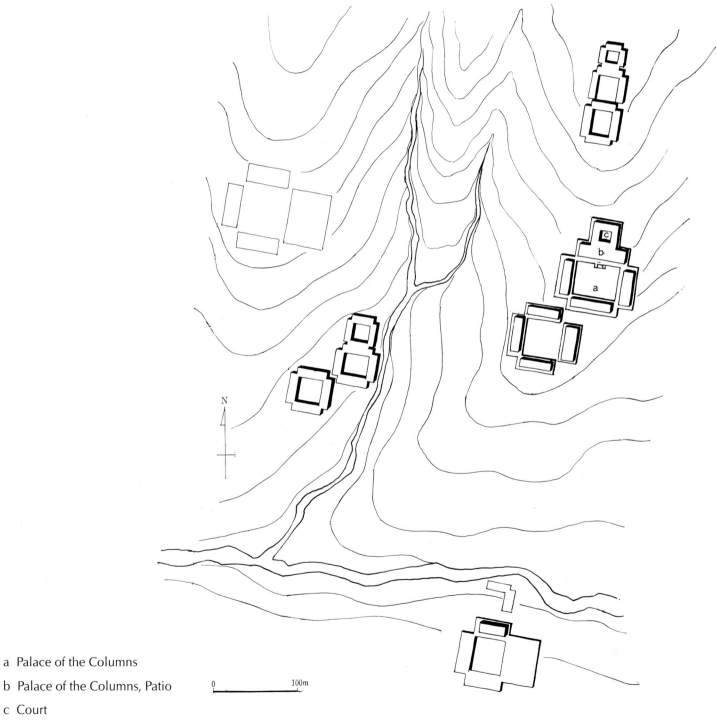

a Palace of the Columns
b Palace of the Columns, Patio
c Court

Detail from an interior court wall showing the astonishing precision of Mitla's stone work.

. . .The monuments of Greece and Rome, in their best time, can alone compare with the splendour of this great edifice. The ornamentation is arranged with perfect symmetry, the joints are carefully cut, the beds and arris of the cornices faultless, showing that the builders were masters of their art. The lintels in this monument consist, like those of Greece and Rome, of large blocks of stone; the ornamentation is a series of varied panels, set in elegant frames, composed of small stones beautifully cut, arranged in meanders, trellis-work, and diversified in combinations. (Viollet-le-Duc, as quoted by Charnay, 1887)

Mitla is unique both in the extreme precision of its forms and in the complete absence of monumental temple-pyramids. Mitla's structures are palace complexes where architectural elegance and control have replaced overwhelming scale as symbols of power.

Contributing to the palace atmosphere are the residential scale, the many courts, and the substantial though dark interior spaces. In spite of the more intimate scale of Mitla, no new relationship is established between interior and exterior space. Even the few doorways, widened with the use of columns, imply by their shape the sense of impenetrable mass. Solid-looking masses and the courts they enclose are static, independent elements. The open or recessed corners of the groups create actual or implied separation of each building which enables visual correction of the long rectangular forms through articulated corners and the slight negative batter of the walls.

Enclosing the north side of the main plaza is the magnificent Palace of the Columns (64-69) named for the great hall of gigantic columns that supported wooden beams and a flat roof of twigs and plaster (68).

The building arrangement and the stone mosaics resemble Mayan Uxmal's Nunnery, but at Mitla the patterns are strictly geometric and everything is much more meticulously executed. Mitla's particular forms, extreme precision, and skillful masonry have no known direct antecedents.

It is not, however, a radical departure from tradition but a place where many of the fundamental tendencies of New World architecture have been gathered in a matchless composition of complexity and control.

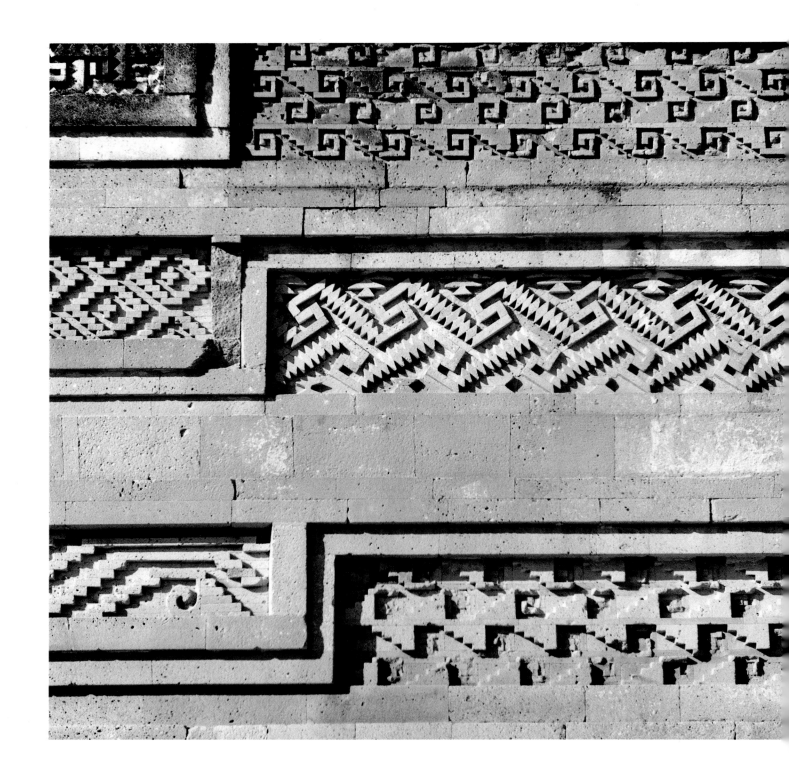

The intricate and precise weaving motifs covering every facade were made of interlocking individual stones that stood out from a background of brightly colored stucco. West end of the Palace of the Columns and a detail (70, 71).

Interior corner of the courtyard in the Palace of
the Columns.

market at Tula (28). The Mayans, on the other hand, employed wood only as door lintels and unstructurally in their corbelled masonry vaulting system (156). The corbelled vaults required massive stabilizing walls and enormous height for short spans limiting Mayan interiors to cramped, narrow spaces with few openings (90). The impressive spaces in the New World, as befits their ceremonial intent, were not interior rooms but exterior stages—the plazas and court yards defined by impressive facades and soaring pyramids.

City Types and Planning

Clearly these were not cities in the modern sense—not the dense, bustling urban areas that the word city means to us. Instead, with one or two notable exceptions, they were primarily ceremonial and administrative centers, the focus of a largely dispersed population. Undoubtedly they were also market centers where, either regularly or at festivals, people would gather from a wide area to trade—just as happens today in this part of the world.

They were the prototype city, a place deliberately meant to awe and overpower the beholder. Their impact was from large brilliantly colored forms parting the jungle or capping a plateau. These cities did not require the sophistication of Greek or Egyptian architecture to fulfill their purpose; their splendor was that they existed and their existence required only the simplest geometry to separate them sharply from the background and from the everyday experience of the people. In an often overpowering landscape these cities focused the thinly scattered populace, their imposing forms marking one place where man appeared to control his destiny and where each generation could fulfill its wish for immortality.

The principal building types are few. In addition to the dominant temple-pyramids and platforms of obvious religious purpose, most cities include a variety of additional structures whose precise use, except for the ball courts, can only be surmised. The names by which they are called today are merely convenient or legendary.

With the striking exception of Teotihuacan (12-13) and parts of Tikal (84-85), buildings were

If the number, grandure and beauty of its buildings were to count toward the attainment of renown and reputation in the same way as gold, silver and riches have done for other parts of the Indies, Yucatan would have become as famous as Peru and New Spain have become, so many, in so many places, and so well built of stone are they, it is a marvel; the buildings themselves, and their number are the most outstanding thing that has been discovered in the Indies. (Friar Diego de Landa, 1570)

Before the Spaniards subdued the country the Indians lived together in well ordered communities; they kept the ground in excellent condition, free from noxious vegetation and planted with fine trees. The habitation was as follows: in the center of the town were the temples, with beautiful plazas, and around the temples stood the houses of the chiefs and the priests, and next those of the leading men. Closest to these came the houses of those who were wealthiest and most esteemed, and at the borders of the town were the houses of the common people. The wells, where they were few, were near the house of the chiefs; their plantations were set out in the trees for making wine, and sown with cotton, pepper, and maize . . . . (Friar Diego de Landa, 1570)

I am entering abruptly upon new ground. Volumes without number have been written to account for the first peopling of America. By some the inhabitants of this continent have been regarded as a separate race, not descended from the same common father with the rest of mankind; others have ascribed their origin to some remnant of the antediluvian inhabitants of the earth, who survived the deluge which swept away the greatest part of the human species in the days of Noah, and hence have considered them the most ancient race of people on the earth. Under the broad range allowed by a descent from the sons of Noah, the Jews, the Canaanites, and Phoenicians, the Cathaginians, the Greeks, the Scythians in ancient times; the Chinese, the Swedes, the Norwegians, the Welsh, and the Spaniards in modern, have had ascribed to them the honour of peopling America. The two continents have been joined together and rent asunder by the shock of an earthquake; the fabled island of Atlantis has been lifted out of the ocean; and, not to be behindhand, an enterprising American has turned the tables on the Old World, and planted the ark itself within the State of New-York.

The monuments and architectural remains of the aborigines have heretofore formed but little part of the groundwork for these speculations. Dr. Robertson, in his History of America, lays it down as "a certain principle, that America was not peopled by any nation of the ancient continent which had made considerable progress in civilization." "The inhabitants of the New World," he says, "were in a state of society so extremely rude as to be unacquainted with those arts which are the first essays of human ingenuity in its advance toward improvement." Discrediting the glowing accounts of Cortez and his companions, of soldiers, priests, and civilians, all concurring in representations of the splendour exhibited in the buildings of Mexico, he says that the "houses of the people were mere huts, built with turf, or mud, or the branches of trees, like those of the rudest Indians." The temple of Cholula was nothing more than "a mound of earth, without any steps or any facing of stone, covered with grass and shrubs;" and, on the authority of persons long resident in New Spain, and who professed to have visited every part of it, he says that "there is not, in all the extent of that vast empire, a single monument the vestige of any building more ancient than the conquest." At that time, distrust was perhaps the safer side for the historian; but since Dr. Robertson wrote a new flood of light has poured upon the world, and the field of American antiquities has been opened. (John Lloyd Stephens, 1841)

seldom composed into any overriding processional or hieratic spatial order. Instead, by their irregular, multi-level placement, by the freedom from a rigid overall symmetry, the importance and individuality of each were emphasized. These individual, solid masses were the positive elements of the composition and space became what was left over, staked out by free and emphatic forms.

Despite an overall asymmetry, groups as well as individual buildings were nearly always, if loosely, axially ordered. This local symmetry further emphasized the self-contained quality of individual structures. Deliberate or not, part of the explanation for a lack of overall order was the growth of these cities by accretion as over generations buildings were added or enlarged and concepts or plans superseded and revised.

Only at Teotihuacan does a strong axial order appear to have been imposed initially and all later building ordered by it. One can clearly see at Teotihuacan how such order tightens the relationship of the various structures in space, reduces their individuality, and emphasizes the importance of echoing rhythms. The whole composition assumes greater importance than its parts. Perhaps the original architects sensed that the scale of the Mexican landscape at Teotihuacan demanded this vast geometry which resulted in the largest spatial composition ever conceived by man.

Architectural Form

As this architecture now exists with colors faded and the stucco gone, its initial effect and sense of monumentality are enhanced by the visible weight of piled up stone—a sense of structure and process not an integral part of the original. The use of weight-destroying stucco covering meant that the effect depended on sheer size, vividness of color, and articulation of form. The development of New World architecture reveals an increasing concern for the nuances of their basic shapes. There is growing awareness of how expressive silhouette actually and mystically separates mass from environment and experience; of how clearly defined and exaggerated corners strengthen simpler lines and planes between and optically sharpens the total form; of how the insistent horizontality of line, plane, and shadow unify form; and of how carefully proportioned and contained decoration not only astounds the eye but increases the visual separation of facade planes.

The importance of this stepped, hovering horizontality in creating a sense of solidity and weight can be seen by contrasting the smooth stuccoed shapes of Zacaleu (126-131) with those of Uxmal's Nunnery (167-177).

Mexican Cultures

Central Mexico witnessed a succession of cultures spread over almost two thousand years, each centered around a great city. The wide range of conditions under which these cities were built included the low wet jungles of the east coast, the dry moonscape of the central plateau, and the high pleasant valleys of south central Mexico. In spite of this geographic and climatic range the essential forms and techniques were similar and a remarkable unity exists over immense stretches of space and time.

Strangely enough such unity may be explained in part by the diversity of Mexico's geography and climate; diverse conditions meant a variety of growing seasons, foods, and natural materials that encouraged trade between regions resulting in the rapid spread of ideas, art, and technology.

The Maya

Mayan traditions, which began in one of the world's rainiest regions, were initially softer and more sculptural. Mexican forms under the influence of the clear dry light of the Mexican plateau, from the beginning, had a greater precision of form and crispness of edge. This same precision increased in Mayan architecture as it moved into the harsh light of Yucatan. In both areas, however, the conflict between the more precise geometry implied by the masonry and the freer plasticity allowed by the stucco is evident. Early the plastic qualities of the heavy stucco dominated and only later, as stone cutting became more skillful and stucco thinned and articulate form became of increased concern, did the precision of the masonry assert itself.

Actual contacts between the Mayan and Mexican areas, even the mutual penetration of architectural styles, appears to have occurred frequently, but in general the Mayans enjoyed a long uninterrupted history and developed their own distinctive architecture—which later influenced styles at Mexican sites such as Xochicalco (54-61).

The climatic and geographic conditions of Mayan cities although not as varied, were in many ways more severe than those in Mexico. On the surface the Mayans appear to have developed cities in some of the most unlikely spots in history such as the sites near Tikal in the middle of the Peten jungle. Later cities were founded to the south at Copan, to the west in the Guatemalan highlands and the Usumacinta River valley, and finally north into the dry scrub jungle of the Yucatan peninsula.

Despite the variety of cultures, geography and climate, it is not surprising to find an underlying unity to Mexican and Mayan architecture. Linked by extensive trade and eventually conquest, the cultures, the functional requirements, and the technological means were remarkably similar.

The first new light thrown upon this subject as regards Mexico was by the great Humboldt, who visited that country at a time when, by the jealous policy of the government, it was almost as much closed against strangers as China is now. No man could have better deserved such fortune. At that time the monuments of the country were not a leading object of research; but Humboldt collected from various sources information and drawings, particularly of Mitla, or the Vale of the Dead; Xoxichalco, a mountain hewed down and terraced, and called the Hills of Flowers; and the great pyramid or Temple of Cholula he visited himself, of all which his own eloquent account is within reach of the reader. Unfortunately, of the great cities beyond the Vale of Mexico, buried in forests, ruined, desolate, and without a name, Humboldt never heard, or, at least, he never visited them. It is but lately that accounts of their existence reached Europe and our own country. These accounts, however vague and unsatisfactory, had roused our curiosity; though I ought perhaps to say that both Mr. C. and I were somewhat skeptical, and when we arrived at Copan, it was with the hope, rather than the expectation, of finding wonders. *(John Lloyd Stephens, 1841)*

PART II

MAYAN CITIES
TIKAL
COPAN
PALENQUE
ZACALEU
TULUM
XLAPAK
SAYIL
LABNA
KABAH
UXMAL
CHICHEN ITZA

I set out with the proposition that they were not Cyclopean, and do not resemble the works of Greek or Roman; there is nothing in Europe like them. We must look, then to Asia and Africa.

It has been supposed that at different periods of time vessels from Japan and China had been thrown upon the western coast of America. The civilization, cultivation, and science of those countries are known to date back from a very early antiquity. Of Japan I believe some accounts and drawings have been published, but they are not within my reach; of China, during the whole of her long history, the interior has been so completely shut against strangers that we know nothing of her ancient architecture. Perhaps, however, that time is close at hand. At present we know only that they have been a people not given to change; and if their ancient architecture is the same as their modern, it bears no resemblance whatever to these unknown ruins. *(John Lloyd Stephens, 1841)*

Trail in the rain forest near Tikal (77).

TIKAL

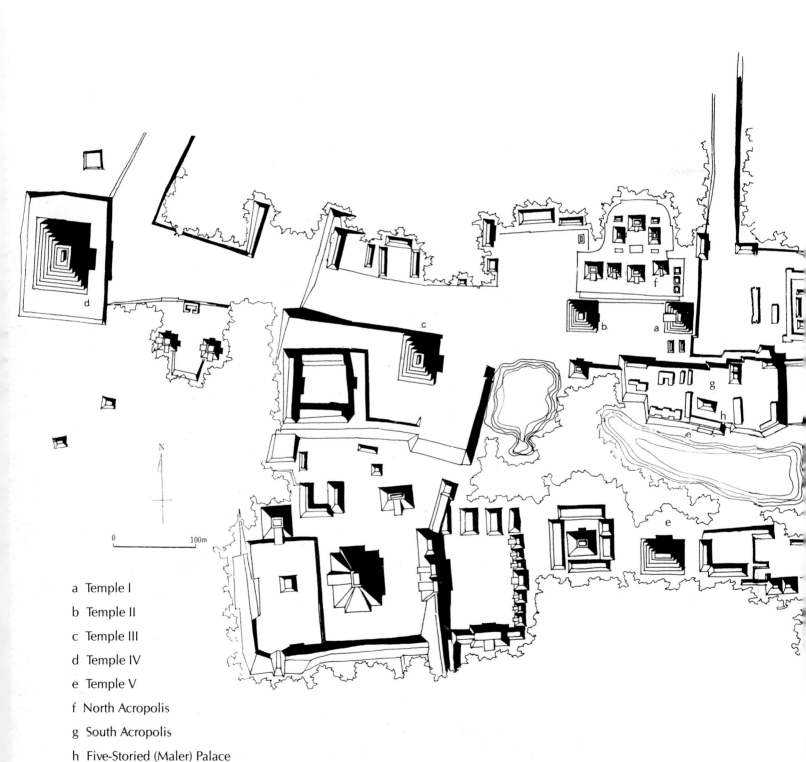

a Temple I

b Temple II

c Temple III

d Temple IV

e Temple V

f North Acropolis

g South Acropolis

h Five-Storied (Maler) Palace

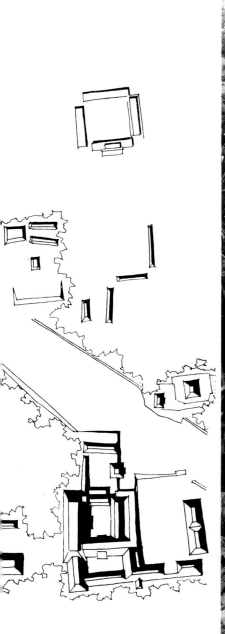

Before clearing, every building at Tikal was overgrown with trees and vines—often the only thing that bound the stones together.

79

Tikal was first stumbled upon by a wandering priest in 1696. A Col. Mendez reconnoitered the site in 1848, but Stephens and Catherwood, despite their extensive travels about the same time, never visited here. Alfred Maudsley, the English archaeologist, photographed and mapped part of the site in 1881 and 1882 and in the early 20th century the eccentric archaeologist—photographer Theobert Maler made some outstanding pictures of partially cleared buildings whetting everyone's appetite for more. Since that time investigations have proceeded on and off hampered by inaccessibility, a difficult climate, and lack of funds. wide ranging and systematic exploration was begun in the late 1950's by the University of Pennsylvania's Edwin Shook, William Coe and their associates. Today most major buildings are cleared and restored so one has a good sense of how this largest Mayan city appeared to its last inhabitants. The photographs show some of these changes over the last twenty five years.

Unless the climate has changed radically during the last thousand years, which appears unlikely, the physical environment of Tikal is one of the most difficult imaginable. In the midst of heavy jungle, miles from any river or lake, rainfall is alternately excessive or nonexistent. Why the Mayans would establish a major city under these conditions is a mystery. One explanation may be the Indian "slash and burn" method of growing corn which needed frequent rotation of fields and the rapid soil replenishment possible in the jungle.

The site contains several large ponds, or cenotes, for water storage; judging from their capacity and the extensive number of house mounds discovered in the surrounding jungle, Tikal at its peak was the center of a dense population. Evidently it suffered an abrupt decline or even abandonment around 900 AD. Many reasons have been cited for the eclipse of this and other jungle cities; disease, uprisings, invasion, soil depletion, and climate change. The true explanation remains a mystery.

Before much restoration work began in the 1960's only the tips of the five major pyramids were visible above the jungle. Temple I, II and III from Temple IV.

The main plaza, from Temple I, at three stages during investigation and restoration: top left, 1960 (soon after work began at Tikal), three pyramids are visible to the west; bottom left, 1965, the top of Temple II has been restored and the plaza cleared; this page, 1986, further restoration of Temple II and the North Acropolis. Note how the large pyramid on the right has been decapitated. This pyramid together with I & II were erected around 700 AD making the Great Plaza the central focus of Tikal.

Central Tikal today seen from the North Acropolis. All five pyramids are visible—Temple V, beyond the main plaza has been left just as it was found (84-85). A smaller, sixth pyramid, the Temple of the Inscriptions, lies some distance to the southeast.

Temples II, III, and IV from Temple I in 1965 (86) and 1986 (87).

Punctuated by its five 140 to 230 foot-high pyramids, ornate and brilliantly colored, floored by vast areas of stucco paving, Tikal was, in that oppressive jungle, a fantastic symbol of power and control.

Construction consisted of a massive rubble core surfaced with limestone and stucco leaving barely usable interior spaces. The effect, as befits its symbolic purpose, was impressive in mass if somewhat crude in detail. Only the elegantly carved wood lintels and a few stelae show a refinement equal to later Maya.

Stela 31, erected about 500 AD and found beneath a mound on the North Acropolis contains signs of central Mexican contact in the image of the rain god Tlaloc on the shield.

Limited by the massive walls and corbeled arch to narrow and high spaces, Peten Mayan interiors are generally only one room deep—beyond that the rooms were too dark and dank. Windows were seldom used— the occasional ventilation slots in the thick masonry seem ineffective. Instead doorways, widened by using wooden lintels, often intricately carved, provided access to light and air.

This uncommonly open space connects shallow rooms on the north and south sides of a palace on the Central Acropolis (89).

The most beautiful interior at Tikal is this room in the Maler Palace—in nearly perfect condition when first photographed by Teobert Maler in 1895. The limited comfort is readily apparent; plastered benches, minimal light and air. Possibly such rooms were temporary quarters only, used by priests or dignitaries during ceremonies. The purpose of the carved wooden poles is unknown but, whether the Mayan builders realized it or not, they are structurally unnecessary, though decorative and handy supports for hanging storage (90-91).

Temple I and Temple II tower over the Great Plaza and its commemorative stelae. Erected during the four hundred years beginning in the 4th century AD, some still show traces of their original red paint (92, 93).

COPAN

Rescued from the river eroding its Acropolis, Copan is a sensitively restored and superbly maintained site. More than anywhere else the beauty of the landscape, the presence of the jungle, and emerging architecture combine to create the authentic atmosphere of a great religious center.

Copan has few free-standing architectural monuments to admire. Instead, moving about the site dominated by the continuous mass of the Acropolis, with its multiple levels, mounds, courts and ever-present forest, or crossing the great plaza marked by colossal idols, is primarily a spatial experience. The existence of these remarkable spaces, however, may be as dependent on the limited restoration as on original concepts. Conceivably, with the magnificent space-defining trees removed and the architecture more fully restored a typical configuration of contained and solid masses would emerge. One cannot deny, however, that intentionally or not, the complexity, scale, and continuity of Copan's forms results in space being a more positive element of the composition than at any other Mayan city.

Despite a lack of outstanding architecture Copan excels in the quality and variety of its sculpture. Most impressive are the many dated stelae arrayed in the Great Plaza to mark important events. The figures and glyphs of these stelae are beautifully carved in typical Mayan style, but other sculpture, such as the full round heads found on the Acropolis, is strangely realistic and alien in feeling.

a Great Plaza

b Ball Court

c Hieroglyphic Stairway

d Acropolis

e Review Stand court

f Rio Copan

The reader is perhaps curious to know how old cities sell in Central America. Like other articles of trade, they are regulated by the quantity in the market and the demand; but, not being staple articles like cotton and indigo, they were held at fancy prices, and at that time were dull of sale. I paid fifty dollars for Copan. There was never any difficulty about price. I offered that sum, for which Don Jose Maria thought me only a fool; if I had offered more, he would probably have considered me something worse. (John Lloyd Stephens, 1841)

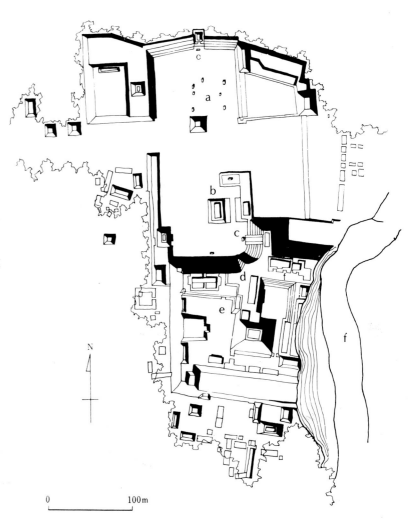

0   100m

...*Our guide cleared a way with his machete, and we passed, as it lay half buried in the earth, a large fragment of stone elaborately sculptured, and came to the angle of a structure with steps on the sides, in form and appearance, so far as the trees would enable us to make it out, like the sides of a pyramid. Diverging from the base, and working our way through the thick woods, we came upon a square stone column, about fourteen feet high and three feet on each side, sculptured in very bold relief, and on all four of the sides, from the base to the top. The front was the figure of a man curiously and richly dressed, and the face, evidently a portrait, solemn, stern, and well fitted to excite terror. The back was of a very different design, unlike anything we had ever seen before, and the sides were covered with hiero-glyphics. This our guide called an "Idol;" and before it, at a distance of three feet, was a large block of stone, also sculptured with figures and emblematical devices, which he called an altar. The sight of this unexpected monument put at rest at once and forever, in our minds, all uncertainty in regard to the character of American antiquities, and gave us the assurance that the objects we were in search of were interesting, not only as the remains of an unknown people, but as works of art, proving, like newly-discovered historical records, that the people who once occupied the Continent of America were not savages. With an interest perhaps stronger than we had ever felt in wandering among the ruins of Egypt, we followed our guide, who, sometimes missing his way, with a constant and vigorous use of his machete, con-ducted us through the thick forest, among half-buried fragments, to fourteen monuments of the same character and appearance, some with more elegant designs, and some in workmanship equal to the finest monuments of the Egyptians; one displaced from its pedestal by enormous roots; another locked in the close embrace of branches of trees, and almost lifted out of the earth; another hurled to the ground, and bound down by huge vines and creepers; and one standing, with its altar before, in a grove of trees which grew around it, seemingly to shade and shroud it as a sacred thing; in the solemn stillness of the woods, it seemed a divinity mourning over a fallen people. (John Lloyd Stephens, 1841)*

Stelae F, B, E, C, 8 to 12 feet high, were erected in the Great Plaza between 600 and 800 AD (95).

North face of the Acropolis (97). From the Acropolis one overlooks the Ball Court and, beyond, the Great Plaza in which stand many magnificent stelae (98).

Unique stepped, corbeled arch of the Ball Court buildings (100). The Hieroglyphic Stairway leading to the top of a former pyramid (99, 101).

So-called Reviewing Stand, Western Court of the Acropolis (102) adorned with a monkey-faced figure holding a sceptre incised with the 'T' Ik sign, meaning wind (103t).

Nearby is this large date glyph recording a count of 13 periods (two bars of 5 and 3 dots of 1 each), (103b).

Ball Court and Acropolis from the Great Plaza with stelae F, H, and altars (105).

Climbing over the ruined top, we reached a terrace over-grown with trees and, crossing it, descended by stone steps into an area so covered with trees that at first we could not make out its form. When the machete had cleared the way, we saw that it was a square with steps on all the sides almost as perfect as those of the Roman amphitheatre. The steps were ornamented with sculpture, and on the south side, about halfway up, forced out of its place by roots, was a colossal head, again evidently a portrait. We ascended these steps and reached a broad terrace a hundred feet high overlooking the river and supported by the wall which we had seen from the opposite bank. The whole terrace was covered with trees, and even at this height were two gigantic ceibas (kapok trees), over twenty feet in circumference; their half-naked roots extended fifty or a hundred feet around, binding down the ruins and shading them with their wide-spreading branches.

We sat down on the very edge of the wall and strove in vain to penetrate the mystery by which we were surrounded. Who were the people that built this city? In the ruined cities of Egypt, even in the long-lost Petra, the stranger knows the story of the people whose vestiges he finds around him. America, say historians, was peopled by savages; but savages never reared these structures, savages never carved these stones. When we asked the Indians who had made them, their dull answer was "Quien sabe?" "Who knows?" There were no associations connected with this place, none of those stirring recollections which hallow Rome, Athens, and "The world's great mistress on the Egyptian plain." But architecture, sculpture, and painting, all the arts which embellish life, had flourished in this overgrown forest; orators, warriors, and statesmen, beauty, ambition, and glory had lived and passed away, and none knew that such things had been, or could tell of their past existence. Books, the records of knowledge, are silent on the theme.

The city was desolate. No remnant of this race hangs round the ruins, with traditions handed down from father to son and from generation to generation. It lay before us like a shattered bark in the midst of the ocean, her masts gone, her name effaced, her crew perished, and none to tell whence she came, to whom she belonged, how long on her voyage, or what caused her destruction—her lost people to be traced only by some fancied resemblance in the construction of the vessel, and, perhaps, never to be known at all. The place where we were sitting, was it a citadel from which an unknown people had sounded the trumpet of war? or a temple for the worship of the God of peace? or did the inhabitants worship idols made with their own hands and offer sacrifices on the stones before them? All was mystery, dark, impenetrable mystery, and every circumstance increased it. In Egypt the colossal skeletons of gigantic temples stand in unwatered sands in all the nakedness of desolation; but here an immense forest shrouds the ruins, hiding them from sight, heightening the impression and moral effect, and giving an intensity and almost wildness to the interest. (John Lloyd Stephens, 1841)

PALENQUE

Palenque, as one early explorer wrote, is poised like an unshed tear at the edge of the vast Chiapas mountains, its silvery towers visible for miles across the plains below that stretch to Yucatan. The builders of Palenque freely adapted these rolling foothills to their purposes. And, as if compelled by the beauty of the place, they also set about to transform the heavy monumentality of the jungle cities. Openings were drastically increased, walls thinned, and roofs mansarded. Human-scaled, livable spaces were incorporated into the Palace complex along with courts, cloisters and a watchtower.

As the ruins of Palenque are the first which awakened attention to the existence of ancient and unknown cities in America, and as, on that account, they are perhaps more interesting to the public, it may not be amiss to state the circumstances of their first discovery.

In the year 1750, a party of Spaniards traveling in the interior of Mexico penetrated to the lands north of the district of Carmen in the province of Chiapas, when all at once they found, in the midst of a vast solitude, ancient store buildings, the remains of a city still embracing from eighteen to twenty-four miles in extent, which was known to the Indians by the name of Casas de Piedras.

The existence of such a city was entirely unknown; there is no mention of it in any book, and no tradition that it had ever been. To this day it is not known by what name it was called, and the only appellation given to it is that of Palenque, after the village near which the ruins stand.
(John Lloyd Stephens, 1841)

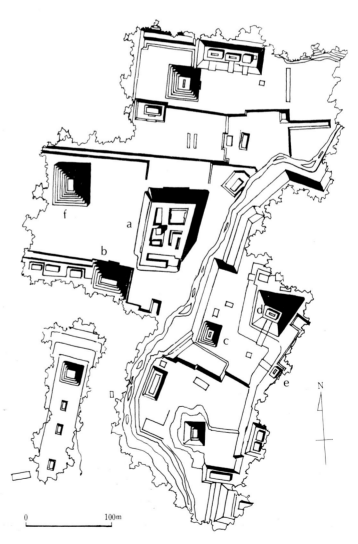

a Palace

b Temple of the Inscriptions

c Temple of the Sun

d Temple of the Cross

e Temple of the Foliated Cross

f Pyramid

Aerial view of Palenque (1986) from the north. The site from pyramid (f) as the morning mists, so frequent at Palenque, begin to rise (108-109).

This important city is apparently without civic architecture; no public buildings are found, there seems to have been nothing but temples and tombs. Consequently the great edifice was not a royal palace but rather a priestly habitation, a magnificent convent occupied by the higher clergy of this holy centre, as the reliefs everywhere attest.

Had Palenque been the capital of an empire, the palace a kingly mansion, the history of her people, fragments of domestic life, pageants, recitals of battles and conquests, would be found among the reliefs which everywhere cover her edifices, as in Mexico, at Chichen Itza, and other cities in Yucatan; whereas the reliefs in Palenque show nothing of the kind. On them we behold peaceful stately subjects, usually a personage standing with a scepter, sometimes a calm, majestic figure whose mouth emits a flame, emblem of speech and oratory. They are surrounded by prostrated acolytes, whose bearing is neither that of slaves nor of captives; for the expression of their countenance, if submissive, is open and serene, and their peaceful attitude indicates worshippers and believers; no arms are found among these multitudes, nor spear, nor shield, nor bow, nor arrow, nothing but the preachers and devotees.

The interest attaching to these studies is certainly profound and sincere, yet it does not entirely banish the consciousness of our very arduous life among the ruins. The rain is incessant; the damp seems to penetrate the very marrow of our bones; a vegetable mould settles on our hats which we are obliged to brush off daily; we live in mud, and we are covered with mud, we breathe in mud, whether amongst the ruins or wandering away from them; the ground is so slippery that we are as often on our backs as on our feet. (Desire Charnay, 1887)

No rest for the explorer, is the fiat that has gone forth. At night the walls, which are covered with greenish moss, trickle down on our weary heads and awake us out of our sleep; in the day-time we are prey to swarms of insects, rodadores, mosquitoes, and garrapatas......yet it sinks into utter insignificance as compared with the great joy of our discoveries, the ever fresh interest of our photographs, the looking forward with immense satisfaction to the time when we shall produce the splendid squeezes of these grand, mysterious inscriptions, not yet found in any museum. Well weighed together, these things are calculated to make us forget the hardships and troubles of the moment. (Desire Charnay, 1887)

The road was a mere Indian footpath; the branches of the trees, beaten down and heavy with the rain, hanging so low that we were obliged to stoop constantly; very soon our hats and coats were perfectly wet. From the thickness of the foliage the morning sun could not dry up the deluge of the night before. The ground was very muddy, broken by streams swollen by the early rains, with gullies, in some places very difficult to cross, in which the mules floundered and stuck fast. Amid all the wreck of empires, nothing ever spoke so forcibly of the world's mutations as this immense forest shrouding what was once a great city. Once it had been a great highway, thronged with people who were stimulated by the same passions that give impulse to human action now, but they were all gone, their habitations buried, and no traces of them left.

In two hours we reached the River Micol, and in half an hour more that of Otula, darkened by the shade of the woods and breaking beautifully over a stony bed. Fording this, very soon we saw masses of stones, and then a round sculptured stone. We spurred up a sharp ascent of fragments, so steep the mules could barely climb it, to a terrace which, like the whole road, was so covered with trees it was impossible to make out the form. Continuing on this terrace, we stopped at the foot of a second when our Indians cried out El palacio (The palace), and through openings in the trees we saw the front of a large building richly ornamented with stuccoed figures on the pilasters, curious and elegant, with trees growing close against it, their branches entering the doors; in style and effect it was unique, extraordinary, and mournfully beautiful. (John Lloyd Stephens, 1841)

Temple of the Cross (110, 124-125).

Pyramids in the Americas have been generally
regarded as merely monumental bases for temples.
However, in 1952, deep within the Temple of the
Inscriptions an elaborate tomb and sarcophagus were
uncovered—apparently the burial place of Palenque's
ruler, Lord Pacal who died in 683 AD (112-113).

*Palace complex and tower (114-117). The purpose
of the curious tower is unknown—perhaps it was simply
a watchtower or the whim of some ruler (114-117).*

There was no necessity for assigning to the ruined city an immense extent, or an antiquity coeval with that of the Egyptians or of any other ancient and known people. What we had before our eyes was grand, curious, and remarkable enough. Here were the remains of a cultivated, polished, and peculiar people, who had passed through all the stages incident to the rise and fall of nations, had reached their golden age, and had perished, entirely unknown. The links connecting them with the human family were severed and lost; these were the only memorials of their footsteps upon earth. We lived in the ruined palace of their kings; we went up to their desolate temples and fallen altars; and wherever we moved we saw evidences of their taste, their skill in arts, their wealth and power. In the midst of desolation and ruin we looked back to the past, cleared away the gloomy forest, and fancied every building perfect, with its terraces and pyramids, its sculptured and painted ornaments, grand, lofty, and imposing, and overlooking an immense inhabited plain. We called back into life the strange people who gazed at us in sadness from the walls; pictured them, in fanciful costumes and adorned with plumes of feathers, ascending the terraces of the palace and the steps leading to the temples. Often we imagined a scene of unique and gorgeous beauty and magnificence, realizing the creations of oriental poets, the very spot which fancy would have selected for the "Happy Valley" of Rasselas. In the romance of the world's history nothing ever impressed me more forcibly than the spectacle of this once great and lovely city, overturned, desolate, and lost; discovered by accident, overgrown with trees for miles around, it did not have even a name to distinguish it. Apart from everything else, it was a mourning witness to the world's mutations. (John Lloyd Stephens, 1841)

Although Palenque's underlying masonry was crude, the thick stucco surface was skillfully molded into a variety of flowing decorative forms, especially in panels flanking the temple doorways. Most exterior stucco has badly disintegrated. However, rescued and placed in the small museum at the site are superb specimens of molded stucco and carved stone—elegant testimony to Palenque's release from oppressive monumentalism and to the aura of refined humanity that has appealed to visitors for centuries.

Stone relief from the Palace courtyard (118, 115). Carved glyphs in museum (119). In the lower glyph, the Lord has his arm around his demonic companion and gestures as if to say—"I would like you to meet my friend. . ."

Tablet of the 96 hieroglyphs, an extraordinarily beautiful example of Palenque art marking the ascension of Lord Kuk to the throne in 764 AD (120t). Panel of the Slaves, Palenque Museum (120b).

Stucco head with idealized Mayan features, found in the Temple of Inscriptions tomb, now in the Anthropological Museum, Mexico City (121). Stucco date glyphs, Palenque Museum (121b).

Highest of three temples on eastern edge of Palenque, the Temple of the Foliated Cross's front wall has collapsed revealing several variations of openings including the novel keyhole shape (122).

The Temple of the Sun is regarded as the finest Palenque-style building. The doors are framed with decorative stucco panels as is the sloping roof. On top the remnant of a roof comb adds impressive height to the building without the need for massive masonry. The inner room's rear wall holds a sculpted panel similar to the one on page 120b (123).

Roof comb of the Temple of the Cross with fragments of the stucco covering still clinging to the armature—powerful, abstract sculpture in its own right (124-125).

ZACALEU

A small highland site in northern Guatemala, Zacaleu is the only group where the original stucco surface has been fully restored. The restoration clearly establishes the primary purpose of Mayan cities as settings for religious pageantry. In addition, the rebuilding indicates how the sense of weight implied by the naked masonry masses is almost entirely negated by the stucco surfacing. The plain surfaces however, in their present undecorated simplicity are strangely satisfying. Is it because, to the modern eye, the whole site with its echoing rhythms of steppes and stairways and flowing stucco surface becomes large abstract sculpture?

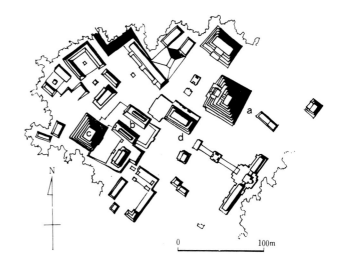

a Central Pyramid

b Ball Court

Central pyramid and nearby buildings.

The site of the ancient city, as at Patinamit and Santa Cruz del Quiche, was chosen for its security against enemies. It was surrounded by a ravine, and the general character of the ruins is the same as at Quiche, but the hand of destruction has fallen upon it more heavily. The whole is a confused heap of grass-grown fragments. The principal remains are two pyramidal structures. . .One of them measures at the base one hundred and two feet; the steps are four feet high and seven feet deep, making the whole height twenty-eight feet. They are not of cut stone as at Copan, but of rough pieces cemented with lime, and the whole exterior was formerly coated with stucco and painted. On the top is a small square platform, and at the base lies a long slab of rough stone, apparently hurled down from the top, perhaps the altar on which human victims were extended for sacrifice. (John Lloyd Stephens, 1841)

The central portion of Zacaleu with the Ball Court in the foreground and the central pyramid beyond— looking, in all its stark simplicity, a little too much like the abandoned set of a low budget Hollywood epic.

TULUM

Tulum may have been the first city in the New World sighted by Spanish ships exploring the east coast of Yucatan in the early 16th century. It was a beautiful site on an otherwise lonely and inhospitable coast, but surrounded by a wall with its back to the sea, Tulum appears to be a last outpost of Mayan civilization and its decadent forms a parody of the great Mayan building tradition.

. . . It is my belief that within this region cities like those we have seen in ruins were kept up and occupied for a long time, perhaps one or two centuries, after the Conquest, and that, down to a comparatively late period, Indians were living in them, the same as before the discovery of America. In fact, I conceive it to be not impossible that within this secluded region may exist at this day, unknown to white men, a living aboriginal city, occupied by relics of the ancient race, who still worship in the temples of their fathers. (John Lloyd Stepens, 1843)

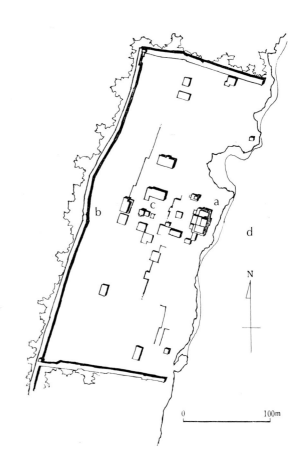

a The Castle, el Castillo

b Main Gate of city wall

c Temple of the Frescoes

d The sea

...We were amid the wildest scenery we had yet found in Yucatan; and, besides the deep and exciting interest of the ruins themselves, we had around us what we wanted at all the other places, the magnificence of nature. Clearing away the platform in front (of the Castillo), we looked over an immense forest; walking around the moulding of the wall, we looked out upon the boundless ocean, and deep in the clear water at the foot of the cliff we saw gliding quietly by a great fish eight or ten feet long.

...(the sea wall of the Castillo) rises on the brink of a high, broken, precipitous cliff, commanding a magnificent ocean view and a picturesque line of coast, being itself visible from a great distance at sea. The wall is solid and has no doorways or entrances of any kind, nor even a platform around it. At evening, when the work of the day was ended and our men returned to the hut, we sat down on the moulding of the wall, and regretted that the doorways of our lofty habitation had not opened upon the sea. Night, however, wrought a great change in our feelings. An easterly storm came on, and the rain beat heavily against the sea wall. We were obliged to stop up the oblong openings, and congratulated ourselves upon the wisdom of the ancient builders. The darkness, the howling of the winds, the cracking of branches in the forest, and the dashing of angry waves against the cliff gave a romantic interest, almost a sublimity to our occupation of this desolate building... (John Lloyd Stephens, 1843)

View from the top of the Castle (133) and of Tulum's site at the edge of the sea (134).
Panorama of central Tulum with Temple of the Frescos (140) in the middle foreground (136).

135

Plaza and grand staircase of the Castle (138), which presents an impenetrable face to the sea (139).

Details of the Temple of the Frescos, a sculpted corner, the gallery and its partially restored fresco of strong Mexican influence (140).

Overgrown main entrance through Tulum's outer wall in the days when it was still a remote outpost on the Yucatan coast (141).

THE PUUC

The Puuc style of Mayan architecture, named for an isolated group of hills at the center of the Yucatan peninsula, includes scores of sites scattered in the scrub jungle. Other than the premier Puuc city, Uxmal, only a bare half dozen of the most accessible sites are cleared and maintained—others slowly crumble away.

Puuc centers flourished from 600-900 AD, appearing suddenly where previously only scattered villages existed; in a great burst of activity temples and palaces were constructed and then mysteriously abandoned.

Why such a concentration of towns and population in this region? Water is scarce except for subterranean cenotes—the agricultural potential is limited (the region today is nearly deserted)—and yet the population may have reached tens of thousands in the villages surrounding Puuc ceremonial centers. The dispersal of Puuc towns may have been in reaction to the suffocating concentration of Peten Maya cities such as Tikal, or merely for more convenient access to land and water. One important technological development was the invention of the man-made cisterns called chultunes—found in many Puuc sites.

Puuc architecture, surprisingly sophisticated and consistent, produced many monumental structures within a short time. It is a style characterized by facades divided horizontally into zones of base, plain lower walls and elaborate friezes of stone mosaic, capped by sharply projecting upper cornices and flat roofs—though roof combs were occasionally used. Mixed with this are a few examples of extremely ornate buildings in the neighboring Chenes style.

The buildings of the Puuc are the last pure Mayan architecture and include some of its finest achievements. It is here that Mayan stone masonry develops the precision that allows its use as a finely cut veneer. The precision of the veneer in turn allows the stucco to be radically thinned or eliminated entirely. Along with this new technique is a new emphasis on sharpness of edge and clarity of form that may be a reaction to the hard clear light of Yucatan. Decorated facades, until then mainly soft-edged stucco, became large scale stone mosaics and, as a means of manipulating light and shade became simultaneously more extensive and more geometric. The motivations or symbolic meanings of most of the decoration are unknown, but it has several architectural effects. First, decoration obviously enriches large areas of otherwise blank surface and sets the underlying pattern for coloration of the facades. Second, its spellbinding textures and rhythms increase the sense of monumental presence and magnificence. Third, within the limited vocabulary of Mayan architecture change in decoration was one way similar forms could be strongly varied. Lastly, consciously or not, the slight three dimensionality of the upper facade increases its feeling of weight and of bearing on the plain base, introducing a rudimentary sense of structure to the mass.

Simple Mayan houses at Muna—a style and building technique with ancient antecedents.

Of the many deteriorating buildings once lost
in the forest (144, 145t), a few are being cleared and
partially restored. First photographed by Maler in
1905, Xlapak was still isolated and overgrown in the
1960's. Now rebuilt and accessible, its handsome
frieze can be fully appreciated (145b).

Sayil's partially restored three-storied palace is a fine example of a Puuc-style building (146, 147).

Labna's large rambling 'palace' is the disjointed accumulation from many periods. The Labna detail above is another sample of the Mayan architects' fascination with the articulation and emphasis of a building's corners.

The five-story pyramid/palace at Etzna is capped by a temple replete with roof comb, thereby combining in one structure most major building types in Mayan architecture (150).

A favorite decorative motif, abstracted in stone at Kabah, is the tied-twig wall of the Mayan house (151).

At the distance of two leagues we turned off by a milpa path on the left, and very soon found ourselves among trees, bushes, and a thick, overgrown foliage, which, after the fine open field of Nohpat, we regarded as among the vicissitudes of our fortunes. Beyond we saw through an opening a lofty mound, overgrown, and having upon it the ruins of a building like the House of the Dwarf, towering above every other object, and proclaiming the site of another lost and deserted city. Moving on, again, through openings in the trees, we had a glimpse of a great stone edifice, with its front apparently entire. We had hardly expressed our admiration before we saw another, and at a few horses' length a third. Three great buildings at once, with facades which, at that distance, and by the imperfect glimpses we had of them, showed no imperfection, and seemed entire. We were taken by surprise. Our astonishment and wonder were again roused; and we were almost as much excited as if this was the first ruined city we had seen.

Our guides cut a path for us, and with great difficulty we went on till we found ourselves at the foot of an over-grown terrace in front of the nearest building. Here we stopped; the Indians cleared a place for our horses, we secured them, and, climbing up a fallen wall of the terrace, out of which large trees were growing, came out the platform, and before us was a building with its walls entire, its front more fallen, but the remains showing that it had once been more richly decorated than any at Uxmal. (John Lloyd Stephens, 1841)

Simple facades are characteristic of most buildings at Kabah, the site of what must be the most elaborately decorated walls in all Mayan architecture—the Temple of the Masks, at the center in this Kabah panorama.

The ornaments are of the same character with those at Uxmal, alike complicated and incomprehensible, and from the fact that every part of the facade was ornamented with sculpture, even to the portion now buried under the lower cornice, the whole must have presented a greater appearance of richness than any building at Uxmal. The cornice running over the doorways, tried by the severest rules of art recognized among us, would embellish the architecture of any known era, and, amid a mass of barbarism, of rude and uncouth conceptions, it stands as an offering by American builders worthy of the acceptance of a polished people.

The lintels of the doorways were of wood; these are all fallen, and of all the ornaments which decorated them not one now remains. No doubt they corresponded in beauty of sculpture with the rest of the facade. The whole now lies a mass of rubbish and ruin at the foot of the wall.

On the top is a structure which, at a distance, as seen indistinctly through the trees, had the appearance of a second story, and, as we approached, it reminded us of the towering structures on the top of some of the ruined buildings at Palenque. (John Lloyd Stephens, 1841)

The face of the Temple of the Masks consists of Chac-god masks, each originally with a long hooked nose. Though lacking typical Puuc restraint, the masks are part of a beautifully interwoven pattern well-scaled to the building—a fantastic surface that must have been awe-inspiring to the peasants (152-158, 160).

155

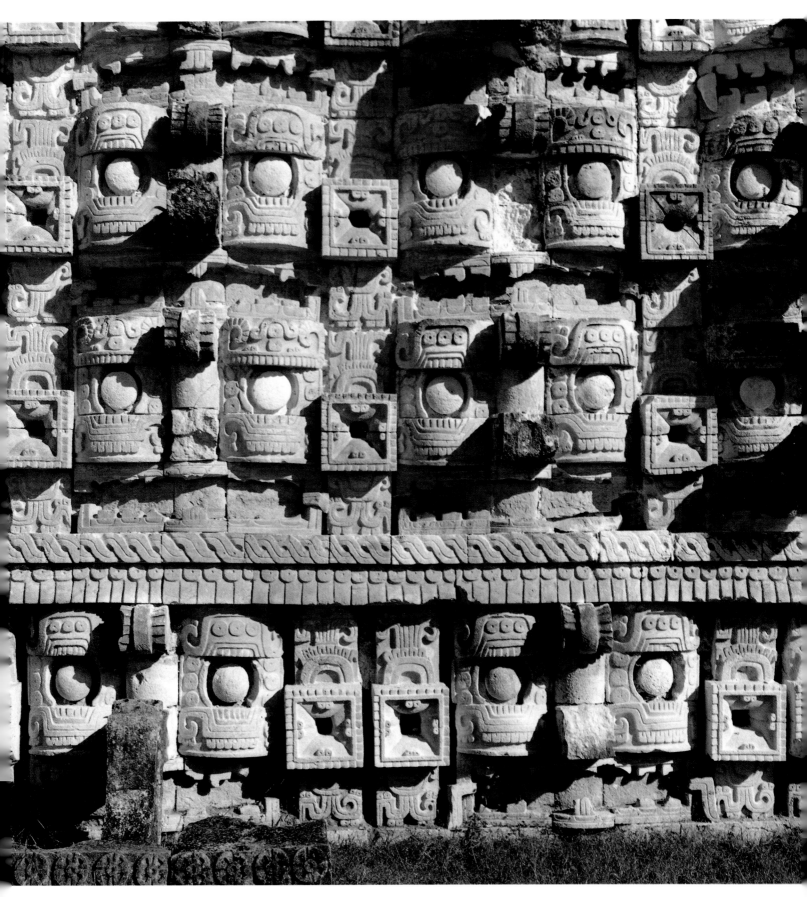

Collapsed end of the Temple of the Masks showing the corbeled construction of the interior rooms, the rubble core, and the method of attaching the facing stones (156).

Detail of the Chac masks (157).

Roof comb of cut stone atop the Temple of the
Masks (158).
Column and capital, Kabah (159).

Kabah. Temple of the Masks' warm colored stone
glowing in the setting sun.

UXMAL

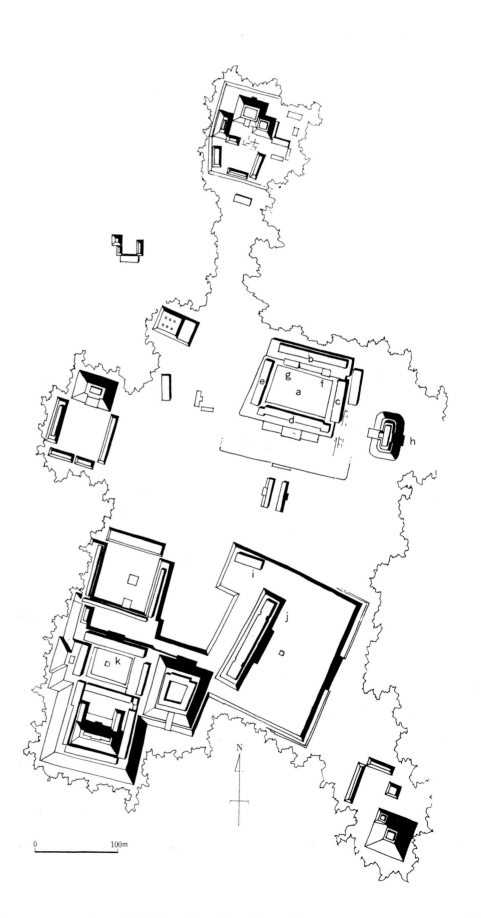

a Courtyard of the Nunnery

b Nunnery, north building

c Nunnery, east building

d Nunnery, south building

e Nunnery, west building

f Nunnery, sub-temple

g Nunnery, sub-temple

h Temple of the Magician pyramid

i House of the Turtles

j Palace of the Governor

k House of the Pigeons

0   100m

Uxmal is the most beautiful of these ancient cities. It is not large nor are its buildings particularly abundant but the siting and high quality of each combine for an impressive effect. Mostly erected during the late Classic Period, Uxmal is the epitome of Puuc and therefore Mayan architecture. It has remained comparatively pure; only a few later additions can be detected such as the rococo Chenes style mask facade on the west side of the pyramid and non-geometric Toltec insertions in a few facades.

Aerial view of Uxmal from the east with the Governor's Palace on the left, the Pyramid of the Magician at the center, and the Nunnery Quadrangle on the right (from 1986).

163

Passing through the arched gateway, we enter a noble courtyard, with four great facades looking down upon it, each ornamented from one end to the other with the richest and most intricate carving known in the art of the builders of Uxmal; presenting a scene of strange magnificence, surpassing any that is now to be seen among its ruins. This courtyard is two hundred and fourteen feet wide, and two hundred and fifty-eight feet deep. At the time of our first entrance it was overgrown with bushes and grass, quails started up from under our feet, and, with a whirring flight, passed over the tops of the buildings. (John Lloyd Stephens, 1841)

. . .These lintels were heavy beams, eight or nine feet long, eighteen or twenty inches wide, and twelve or fourteen thick. The wood, like that at Ococingo, was very hard and rang under the blow of the machete. As our guide told us, it was of a species not found in the neighborhood, but came from the distant forests near the Lake of Peten. Why wood was used in the construction of buildings otherwise of solid stone seemed unaccountable; but if our guide was correct in regard to the place of its growth, each beam must have been carried on the shoulders of eight Indians, with the necessary relief carriers, a distance of three hundred miles; consequently, it was rare, costly, curious, and for that reason may have been considered ornamental. The position of these lintels was most trying, as they were obliged to support a solid mass of stone wall fourteen or sixteen feet high, and three or four in thickness. Once, perhaps, they were strong as stone, but they showed that they were not as durable, and they contained within them the seeds of destruction. Most, it is true, were in their places, sound, and harder than lignum vitae, but others were perforated by wormholes. Some were cracked in the middle, and the walls, settling upon them, were fast overcoming their remaining strength; still others had fallen down altogether. In fact, except in the House of the Nuns the greatest destruction was from the decay and breaking of these wooden beams. If the lintels had been of stone, the principal buildings of this desolate city would at this day be almost entire; or, if the edifices had been still occupied under a master's eye, a decaying beam would have been replaced, and the buildings saved from ruin. At the moment of greatness and power, the builders never contemplated that the time would come when their city would be a desolation. (John Lloyd Stephens, 1841)

Uxmal from the south. The House of the Turtles is at the center and the Nunnery beyond.

The Nunnery Quadrangle, both in general arrangement and in detail, has a strong similarity to the palaces of Mitla. However, the casual relationship of Uxmal's free-standing blocks, together with their variations in height and style, imparts the feeling of a civic plaza rather than a palace complex. The present name stems from the Nunnery's resemblance to a Spanish convent, but more likely it was a forum where each building represented some faction of society—its relative importance indicated by the building's elevation.

The Nunnery Quadrangle from the southeast corner. The plan of the building on the right shows that thinner walls in northern Mayan architecture permit much more usable interiors than the massive Tikal-style.

167

Decorated panels of the north building in the Quadrangle (168-169).

Column detail and interior of the small sub-temple in the Quadrangle. The high proportion of openings to solid wall is exceptional. The column capital, in 'Mayan Doric', shows that the desire for expressive treatment of capitals is nearly universal (170, 171).

The last of the four sides of the courtyard, standing on the right of the entrance, is represented in the plate opposite. It is the most entire of any, and, in fact, wants but little more than its wooden lintels, and some stones which have been picked out of the facade below the cornice, to make it perfect. It is, too, the most chaste and simple in design and ornament, and it was always refreshing to turn from the gorgeous and elaborate masses on the other facades to this curious and pleasing combination. The ornament over the centre doorway is the most important, the most complicated and elaborate, and of that marked and peculiar style which characterizes the highest efforts of these ancient builders. The ornaments over the other doorways are less striking, more simple, and more pleasing. In all of them there is in the centre a masked face with the tongue hanging out, surmounted by an elaborate headdress; between the horizontal bars is a range of diamond-shaped ornaments, in which the remains of red paint are still distinctly visible, and at each end of these bars is a serpent's head, with the mouth wide open. (John Lloyd Stephens, 1841)

The eastern building of the Nunnery Quadrangle was found in near perfect condition and is unusual in the style and simplicity of its mosaic and in the use of alternating latitudinal vaulting expressed in the pattern of the frieze (174-177).

175

Pyramid of the Magician, before the recent restoration of the sloping base.

178

A natural unevenness of site gives prominence to certain elements and may underlie the apparent lack of comprehensive planning. Uxmal's multiple levels and loose arrangement are examples of Puuc concentration on perfection of individual free-standing forms rather than on carefully ordered site planning.

The site looking south from the 100-foot height of the Pyramid of the Magician.

On this third terrace, with its principal doorway facing the range of steps, stands the noble structure of the Casa del Gobernador. The facade measures three hundred and twenty feet. Away from the region of dreadful rains, and the rank growth of forest which smother the ruins of Palenque, it stands with all walls erect and almost as perfect as when deserted by its inhabitants. The whole building is of stone; it is plain up to the moulding that runs along the tops of the doorway, and above it is filled with the same rich, strange, and elaborate sculpture, among which is particularly conspicuous the ornaments before referred to as grecques. There is no rudeness or barbarity in the design or proportions; on the contrary, the whole wears an air of architectural symmetry and grandeur; and as the stranger ascends the steps and casts a bewildered eye along its open and desolate doors, it is hard to believe that he sees before him the work of a race in whose epitaph, as written by historians, they are said to be ignorant of art and to have perished in the rudeness of savage life. If it stood at this day on its grand artificial terrace in Hyde park or the Garden of the Tuileries, it would form a new order, I do not say equaling, but not unworthy to stand side by side with the remains of Egyptian, Greecian, and Roman art. (John Lloyd Stephens, 1841)

Dominating Uxmal by its elevated position and majestic size is the Governor's Palace, the supreme achievement of Mayan architecture, the refinement of its major tenets, and possibly the last work at Uxmal. Its superb proportions are reflected in such details as the vertical relationships of base, plain facade, and decoration; in the breaking of the 300-foot length by indented cross vaults; in the sizing and positioning of the doorways to unify and focus the great facade.

South elevation of Governor's Palace, in excellent condition when first seen by Stephens in 1840's (203).

183

The style and character of these ornaments were entirely different from those of any we had ever seen before, either in that country or any other; they bore no resemblance whatever to those of Copan or Palenque and were quite as unique and peculiar. The designs were strange and incomprehensible, very elaborate, sometimes grotesque, but often simple, tasteful, and beautiful. Among the intelligible subjects are squares and diamonds, with busts of human beings, heads of leopards, and compositions of leaves and flowers, and the ornaments known everywhere as grecques. The ornaments, which succeed each other, are all different, and the whole forms an extraordinary mass of richness and complexity; the effect is both grand and curious. And the construction of these ornaments is no less peculiar and striking than the general effect. There were no tablets or single stones, each representing separately and by itself an entire subject; but every ornament or combination is made up of separate stones, on each of which part of the subject was carved and then set in its place in the wall. Each stone by itself was an unmeaning fractional part; but, placed by the side of others, it helped to make a whole, which, without it, would be incomplete. Perhaps it may, with propriety, be called a species of sculptured mosaic. (John Lloyd Stephens, 1841)

The House of the Turtles, so-called for the turtle motif in the upper cornice. Its simple lines and refined proportions, including even doorway dimensions, have appealed to visitors from Stephens' day to our own, and testify to the sophistication and skill of Uxmal's architects (186, 187).

It stands isolated and alone, seeming to mourn over its own desolate and ruinous condition. With a few more returns of the rainy season it will be a mass of ruins, and perhaps on the whole continent of America there will be no such monument of the purity and simplicity of aboriginal art. (John Lloyd Stephens, 1841)

House of the Pigeons, named for its resemblance to a dove-cote, is in fact the saw-toothed roof comb of a structure largely collapsed (188, 189).

CHICHEN ITZA

a The Nunnery

b The Church

c The Observatory, el Caracol

d The Ball Court

e The Castle pyramid, el Castillo

f Temple of the Warriors

g Market

N

0   100

Chichen Itza, stylistically, is two cities. The northern half with open plazas and martial forms is Toltec-Maya. The older, southern half is Puuc-Maya. The humanly-scaled and casually arranged groups of this southern half are dominated by the circular, free standing Caracol. Believed to have been an observatory since openings in the walls align to important astronomical positions, the Caracol reflects Mayan concern with marking sequences of time. Other groups of the so-called Old Chichen area are scattered in the jungle a mile south of the Caracol.

Aerial view from the south with Mayan Chichen in the foreground, the Ball Court, Castillo, and Warriors of the Toltec-Mayan era in the center and the air-strip beyond (191).

The morning effects of light and shade were no less beautiful; the broad level wrapped in transparent mist, pierced here and there by the pyramids and the wooded eminences, looked like a whitening sea interspersed with green islets; the rising sun, who seemed to create, to raise suddenly into life all the objects touched with his golden wand; presently, like a mighty giant he tore asunder and burnt up the white vapour, and lit up the whole sky. (Desire Charnay, 1887)

Chichen is grouped about two large cenotes or natural wells, the only source of water for most of the year. One of these cenotes has yielded a rich treasure of sacrificed objects. The surrounding plain is flat and featureless scrub jungle.

Dawn from the top of the Nunnery.

At four o'clock we left Piste, and very soon we saw rising high above the plain the Castillo of Chichen. In half an hour we were among the ruins of this ancient city, with all the great buildings in full view, casting prodigious shadows over the plain, and presenting a spectacle which, even after all that we had seen, once more excited in us emotions of wonder. (John Lloyd Stephens, 1841)

The Observatory (El Caracol) and Castillo pyramid (194). Frieze from the upper wall of the Nunnery (195).

Details of the Puuc Mayan-style Nunnery including the ornate Chenes-style 'Church', similar to the small building on Uxmal's pyramid (196, 197, 177).

The Observatory platform and the Red House (198).
The Ball Court, where the object was to get the rubber ball through the hoop. The play may have been for keeps as there is evidence the losers were sacrificed (199).

Northern or Toltec-Maya Chichen from the Ball Court. The strong monumental order of this section contrasts with the more casual Puuc Mayan planning (200-210).

The northern section of the city, with its mixture of central Mexican forms and Mayan skills is the most dramatic and its buildings among the first restored in the New World. The pyramid with its radial symmetry is the pivotal, organizing element of the plaza space which, together with the Ball Court and the Temple of the Warriors, unifies and defines this huge space without confining it. The handsomely proportioned Temple of the Warriors in its profile recalls Teotihuacan, although its reclining Chacmool, serpent columns, and columned market surrounding its base seem a duplication of Tula. In comparison with Tula, the supposed Toltec capital, Chichen both in concept and detail is by far the more impressive; for, at Chichen, Toltec forms and structural innovations are infused with the greater grace and building skill of the Maya.

The expanded architectural possibilities introduced by the Toltecs, had they been allowed a quiet period of gestation, might have spurred Mayan architecture to even greater heights. But the Yucatan peninsula was swept by a long period of disorder and disunity hurrying the collapse of Mayan civilization and bringing to an end Mayan architectural achievement.

And the facility of moving from place to place, were so great, that these could not mar our satisfaction, which was raised to the highest pitch by the ruins themselves. These were, indeed, magnificent. The buildings were large, and some were in good preservation; in general, the facades were not so elaborately ornamented as some we had seen, seemed of an older date, and the sculpture was ruder, but the interior apartments contained decorations and devices that were new to us, and powerfully interesting. All the principal buildings were within a comparatively small compass; in fact, they were in such proximity, and the facilities for moving among them were so great, that by one o'clock we had visited every building, examined every apartment, and arranged the whole plan and order of work. (John Lloyd Stephens, 1841)

Temple of the Warriors from the Castillo (202).

The Castillo; notably, has stairways on four sides, appropriate to its central location in the great north plaza (204, 205).

Temple of the Warriors, reminiscent of Tula (28), where the temple base also is surrounded with a columned hall.

Chacmool altar and feathered serpent columns atop the Temple of the Warriors, Toltec contributions to Chichen (208). Miniature Atlantean figure from the Warriors (209).

Carved jamb from the lower chamber of the Ball Court (210).

A ruin hidden in the bush, once part of greater Chichen which stretches south from the Nunnery (211).

American monuments, considered artistically, are but the rude manifestations of a semi-barbarous race, which it were idle to endow with intrinsic value, seeing their original plans are wanting both in accuracy and symmetry, while their materials are ill-cut, their joints far apart even in bas-reliefs, where the intervening spaces are filled with cement. Consequently these buildings cannot compare with Indian, Egyptian or Assyrian monuments; for here we have a nation who in the whole course of their political life, extending over several centuries, produced but one note, emitted but one sound; because they have neither traditions nor a higher civilization around them to draw from. And, although here and there some happier mood is seen, whether in sculpture or cement modeling, their occurrence is too rare ever to have become general. The chief merit of these buildings lies in their interest for the archaeologist and the intelligent, who are necessarily few; and this explains the silence of the conquerors respecting them . . . . (Desire Charnay, 1887)

Detail, Nunnery Annex, Chichen.

There is, then, no resemblance in these remains to those of the Egyptians; and, failing here, we look elsewhere in vain. The works of these people, as revealed by the ruins, are different from the works of any other known people; they are of a new order, and entirely and absolutely anomalous: they stand alone.

I invite to this subject the special attention of those familiar with the arts of other countries, for, unless I am wrong, we have a conclusion far more interesting and wonderful than that of connecting the builders of these cities with the Egyptians or any other people. It is the spectacle of a people skilled in architecture, sculpture, and drawing, and, beyond doubt, in other more perishable arts; and it possesses the cultivation and refinement attendant upon these, not derived from the Old World, but originating and growing up here, without models or masters, having a distinct, separate, independent existence: like the plants and fruits of the soil, indigenous. (John Lloyd Stephens, 1841)

Carving found near Palenque. In Anthropological Museum, Mexico City.

BIBLIOGRAPHY AND NOTES

A selected group of books out of the hundreds on the subject of Pre-Columbian America. The number is referenced in the text.

Andrews, George. *Maya Cities*. Norman Oklahoma 1975.

Bernal, Ignacio. *Mexico Before Cortez*. New York 1963.

Charnay, Desire. *The Ancient Cities of the New World*. New York 1887.

Coe, William. *Tikal, A Handbook of Ancient Maya Ruins*. Philadelphia 1967.

Coe, Michael. *The Maya*. New York 1984.

Coe, Michael. *Mexico*. New York 1984.

Covarrubias, Miguel. *Indian Art of Mexico and Central America*. New York 1957.

Marquina, Ignacio. *Arquitectura Prehispanica*. Mexico 1951.

1 Kubler, George. *The Art and Architecture of Ancient America*. Baltimore 1962.

Maler, Teobert. Various publications of the Peabody Museum, Harvard. Cambridge 1901-1910.

Morley, Sylvanus G.. *The Ancient Maya*. 3rd edition Stanford 1956.

Proskouriakoff, Tatiana. *An Album of Maya Architecture*. Carnegie Inst., Washington 1946.

Stephens, John Lloyd. *Incidents of Travel in Central America, Chiapas, and Yucatan*. 2 vols. New York 1841.

Stephens, John Lloyd. *Incidents of Travel in Yucatan*. New York 1843.

INDEX

Photographs indicated by ( ).

214

MAP OF MIDDLE AMERICA

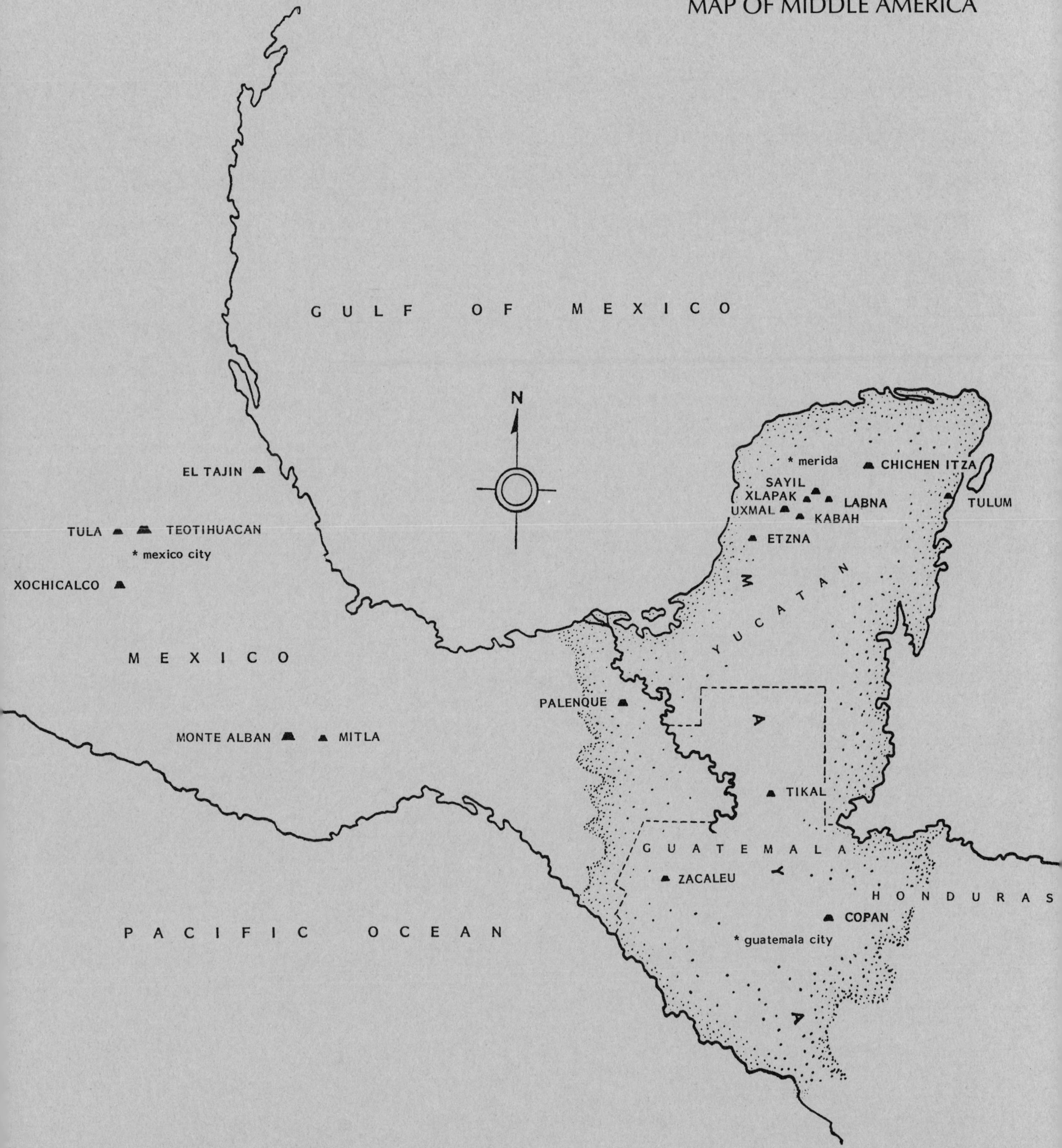

GULF OF MEXICO

N

* merida ▲ CHICHEN ITZA

EL TAJIN ▲

SAYIL ▲
XLAPAK ▲ LABNA ▲
UXMAL ▲ ▲ TULUM
KABAH

TULA ▲ ▲ TEOTIHUACAN

* mexico city

▲ ETZNA

XOCHICALCO ▲

Y
U
C
A
T
A
N

MEXICO

PALENQUE ▲

MONTE ALBAN ▲ ▲ MITLA

▲ TIKAL

GUATEMALA

HONDURAS

▲ ZACALEU

PACIFIC OCEAN

▲ COPAN

* guatemala city

PHOTOGRAPHIC NOTES

The original photographs were made during a series of trips to Mexico and Central America from 1960 to 1965. A great advantage of those days was the relative freedom of access to the sites at all hours. This is now impossible. All sites are now fenced and guarded, opening after and closing before the hours we photographers love best. And for some perverse reason, at many Mexican sites the use of tripods is denied, except by special permit obtainable only in Mexico City, if at all. At Tikal the Guatemalans are more understanding and flexible offering permits to enjoy the sunset from the top of a pyramid.

In the winter of 1986 I revisited many of the sites, courtesy of a pilot friend, in order to make aerial photographs and document restorations completed during the last 20 years.

I used my favorite Hasselblad with lenses from 40mm to 500mm both in the 1960's and now. All new prints were made on Ilford Multigrade, a beautiful full tone and flexible paper.

AVAILABILITY OF PRINTS:

Archival prints made by Norman F. Carver, Jr. of any photograph in this or other of his books are available through the publisher. Prices, as of 1986, are $75 and up depending on size. Please write care of Documan Press Ltd., Box 387, Kalamazoo, MI 49005.